WELCOME TO

I SPY

EASTER

This book belongs to :

Delaney 2023

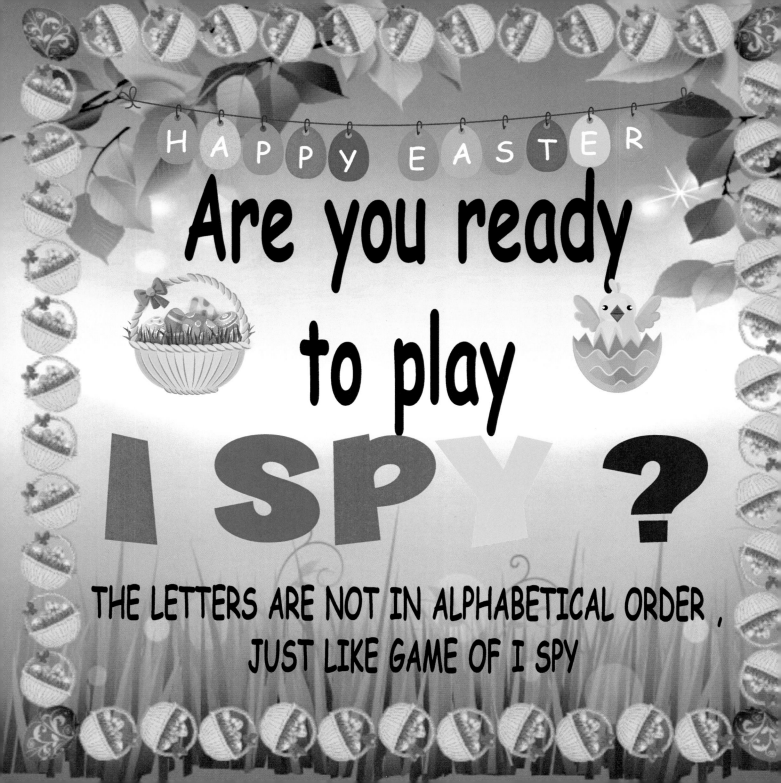

I spy with my little eye something beginning with...

I spy with my little eye something beginning with...

B

B is for Bee

I spy with my little eye something beginning with...

C

C is for Chick

I spy with my little eye something beginning with...

I spy with my little eye something beginning with...

E is for Eggs

I spy with my little eye something beginning with...

F is for

Flowers

I spy with my little eye something beginning with...

G is for Gift

I spy with my little eye something beginning with...

I is for Ice Cream

I spy with my little eye something beginning with...

H is for Hat

I spy with my little eye something beginning with...

K is for King

L is for

Ladybug

I spy with my little eye something beginning with...

J

J is for

Jelly beans

I spy with my little eye something beginning with...

U is for

Unicorn

M is for

Mushrooms

I spy with my little eye something beginning with...

S is for Sweets

I spy with my little eye something beginning with...

P

P is for

Penguin

I spy with my little eye something beginning with...

O is for

Owl

R is for
Rabbit

I spy with my little eye something beginning with...

I spy with my little eye something beginning with...

Made in the USA
Monee, IL
16 March 2023

30023917R00026